A Vacationed Dream

By
Daniel James Glass

Also by Daniel James Glass

Out by Sea, Indefinitely (2019)
Magic Seeds of Personal Destiny (2020)

A Vacationed Dream

By
Daniel James Glass

A Vacationed Dream

www.danieljamesglass.com

ISBN: 978-0-578-85023-8

Cover and book art created by Daniel James Glass

Contents:

A Vacationed Dream is a collection of poetry based on a vacation the author took in the fall of 2020. The book is put together in chronological order of events. Many pieces from this book are written from actual experiences, while others delve into the author's dreams and fantasies about the surrounding Arizona land.

the Night Before

Touch

There is electricity flowing from my fingertips,
making my phone hot to the touch,

and with this tempering buzz
radiating through my body,

I tingle when you touch me,
and I'm even warmer because you love me,

      I lay my head down next to you,
and explore these sparkling electric thoughts
tonight,
      it has been cold here for a little while
but there is a big sun shining stronger down south,

such a wild world, the icicles fall
      when the wind grows strong enough
          to shake the house.

I will be here, rhyming while half asleep
my arms tingling when I shift in the sheets

rolling over these days, they blend together
all of these splintering thoughts appearing
         and disappearing to me.

The notes app on my phone is flooding,
these words are dripping heat,

I've got a fever now, and the melatonin creeps,
otherworldly lessons are flowing into me,

I am recalibrating; I am reexamining
the wild maybes, these trying possibilities

there is always enough to look at
            and to think about,

I have been ready for tomorrow for a little while,
only one more sleep
until we leave

tomorrow we head out
toward wild adventure,
                  and that makes it so hard to sleep.

Waiting for an Avalanche

Waiting for an avalanche
to sweep the mountainside away,
so they can close down this city again
and we will stay inside, only our shadows left to play,

      the air outside is frigid
the cold is shaking the icy sky white,
a snow globe of icicles shaken
      and frozen delight,

      the street lamps glow is mushrooming,
the bar across the street is emptied by the cold,
I'll keep warm underneath these blankets with you
and fall asleep slowly, like the accumulating snow.

Waiting for the snowplows to scrape
and beep in the night,
to do a shitty job
of only removing the uppermost layer of ice,
and leave the asphalt to freeze slick,
      black ice invisible to your sight,

We'll leave at the morning's first light,
with the air making our breathing visible
and my mask worn too tight,
my ears are exposed

to this whispering bite,
we'll leave at sun-up, get out of the freeze,
the sunshine is expecting me
it is all that I need,

all that I need
is a one-story cactus
an Arizona tea,
chiles rellones
with hot cheese,
and skin bright and green,

      a pen and some paper,
some re-occurring nightmare to dream,
because a test of the human heart,
is what this whole damn year
            was for me.

Alarm On

Eyes blinking
　　　　the time

rattling on my wrist
the watch alarms,

open the sky
for the old sun,
open these eyes
slowly in the half-dark,

　　　wake
 big sky, aging eyes,
still black and blue

keep quiet
bird chirps,

I close the front door
and lock it slowly,

it is still early here,
the world rests still,
and here starts
the rest of my life,

warmth is rising from the ground,
       this year is closing up,
like the shortened hours of the café,
before the exit for the airport,

I will break there
before lifting,
on a big bird
in the sky,

the muffin and I both
will crumble in our seat,
falling into another realm,
that starts in my headphones
       and ends in accordion scenes,
of a saguaro cactus standing alone
playing the howling notes
in the Arizona heat,

with a poolside trumpet blaring
the burning notes of the sun lifting my spirit,
       into a desert dream,
my eyes will be sunglassed
and sun-glazed,
       body thirsting,
       for a watered-down retreat
       in a late fall escape,

maybe I will die in the desert, full-bellied,
from a zesty orange muffin
and a cheap poolside, umbrella-ed,
Piña colada shake.

Uber to the Airport

Spanish guitar picking
from old man fingernails,
       tuna boat slinging,
Uber driving captain of the Andrea Gail,

originally from Boston,
he's driven across all 50 states,
an old fish captain turned musician,
and with another San Francisco shipping port delay,
he ran away, and I am running away too
       at least for a few days,

       the resort will be at half capacity
and the airline only serves water for free,
but I've got my audible subscription
cranking in my ears at two and half-speed,

       everyone is moving around
but this planet never moves anywhere,
other than around and around the same star
seemingly fixated in space,

       things are never permanent,
everything in buzzing red at the surface,
earthquakes, fire, death
       and expensive steak,

I am planning to buy desert home décor
    after this extended stay,
    I am astral projecting
to a neighboring star system right now,
and canceling the newspaper deliveries
for this late fall escape
    we call a "getaway."

There are no rules in this place,
there are only laws and consequences.

Neon Sparks

Neon Sparks,
my camera barks,
and spits out
the Polaroid frame

it is a fuzzy image,
sunglasses on my head,
with empty pool chairs
surrounding umbrella-ed shade,

I fall asleep by the pool,
and wake up in a shivering cool,
the towel dampened
but the chill is never entirely removed,

I am not drunk in excuse,
or sunburnt by the afternoon,
I felt the sun's giant rays,
and the humidity today.

Heated visions
of big winded escapes,
my vacationing thoughts
are running away,

vacationed dreams

are never meant for me,
I am still working out
my plan to leave,

another few years
a few moments away,
before I can escape,
like fleeing to the sea

writing nonsense all night,
until the day that I've got an answer,
to poolside poetry dream questions
I have when I am falling asleep,

for these lines of scratch,
are just little cracks,
through the cement streets,
this flower head lifts,

pink and yellow, but not much green
poking through the desert,
each saguaro here
stands tall and unique,

there is a quiet secret,
I can hear but cannot see,
the pool will soon overflow from the rain
falling around these desert dreams.

No, not from a single storm
or a record season of global heat,
there's increasing energy flowing in,
surrounding you and me,

I can feel it buzzing,
like the pink glowing
in the neon hotel sign reading "no vacancy,"

I am alive, time traveling through
a ninety-year lucid dream, making up this life,
gathering paint from the vibrant colors
            in front of me,

I am just a collection of movements,
and the colors I hold and stretch,
from here to where the sun sets,
in Cara Cara orange serenity.

Shots in the Dark

I wish this hotel had a telescope
instead of these poisonous blue drinks,
there are so many stars in the sky tonight,
it gets me wondering about cosmic mysteries
and the lessons these ancient skies could teach,

across the restaurant, they are talking so loud
        that everyone eating at the tables can hear,
            there's a rough rumble echoing
from another round of their cosmopolitan speech,
near a giant caution taped dance floor
the party is out of the scythe's six-foot reach,
        you and I are too,
        we have to sit so far apart
their words are landing heavy near us
they crack off the wall, so crisp and harsh,

        we are only playing games,
there is a handful of missed darts
that were not removed from that back wall,
not even close to where the scoring starts,

        I'm blaming the full moon for it all,
        I put my hands to the spirit in the sky,
        as we alternate throwing out
            our shots in the dark.

Desert Dream # 1

I woke up from a dream
back when this place was alive
with bright street lights shining
over steel accented cars,

I went back in time
to when we were planning
to put men on the moon,
to when this was more than a dive bar,
there was a jukebox blaring Chuck Berry
and not some subscription-based internet Pop radio
          with ads for heartburn relief.

Who would have thought back then,
that it would be so hard for us now
with our world wide web of connection,
to be able to innovate and medicate,
to mediate the global pandemic
we see today, Chuck said it well that
          *"it goes to show
          you never can tell,"*

people used to dance in this parking lot,
before they considered tearing this place down
          before its foundations and floors
          were beginning to give,

there is still magic here now
under these street lights,
        when it is too dark
to see how old this place looks,
too dark, to know what year it is,

a desert hotel retreat from a deserted global disease,
where unless they get a bigger relief paycheck
this place will have to shut down for good,

like some old and tired American dream
the muscle cars still rattle up the roads
I am in this DeLorean dream machine,
time is shaking itself out of order
and glimpses of history appear to me,

it is an American heartache,
a shake shack milkshake heartburn,
a moonshot attempted recovery,
I decide it is time to turn the pillow over
        and fall back asleep.

Tucson and a Phoenix

I spy a firefly
a glass porch door open
       early morning view of Mars
       glowing orange off in the distance,

       I am trying to exist as every color I see,
       a spot of orange is up there
from a flick of the paintbrush
       from a creator's wrist,

       an accidental mark
in the early morning dark sky
       leaving this dancing Phoenix
high in the sky, radio-ing down
       radiated Martian heat,

I am buzzing, entering, and leaving
       this glass porch door view
for I too am an accidental survivor,
       Mr. Trial by Fire,
just a passionate candle spilled
       a big glowing flame,
       that can be seen from far away

I am hoping for the whole sky
       to open orange,

before we leave the hotel
for the day,

on the outskirts of Tucson,
the sunscreen is packed too tightly
in my daughter's unicorn backpack,
and her orange goldfish snacks are crumbling
into my already damaged sunglass frames,

everything is as orange as Mars here
even the mountainside rocks
burn
fiery visions
into my brain.

Suggestion

When you suggested visiting this town
        because the spirits
threw the idea in your head,

        and
you had known nothing
about the town
        I had to go,
                knowing
that you did not know
        why we had to go,

I plan on hash-tagging every photo
        with the sun, a flamingo
        and a cactus,
because of this one million saguaro spread

        that
        is an image
        that no one
        can
                fully
        illustrate.

The Known Unknown

Another dandelion wish,
I will go where this good wind blows me,
I will fly to where I can grow.

The world is full of mystery
filled with beautiful gifts it can show,

there is a lifetime of things due,
                but I feel free
        and feel that I have nothing to prove

I only have Orwell's big brother to destroy
and flowers
        to water twice a day,

I always carry a collection of mixed feelings though
because I have seen oceans devour men,
        trying the tides

people are dying
        for lessons
they should not have to learn,

but that's just part of this life,
people are always living to explore

people are dying to understand
lessons that they
          have always known.

Days Three and Four

Glow

I can sparkle across the night sky,
        wings spread like a butterfly
or a moth sucked into a glowing neon sign,
        little burning flapping meteor,
breaking into a million pieces
        while I fade away,

I can scream like I am reaching God
        el Grito echoing this time
        across eternity,
        your stomach drops
        as I cross this life
        into the ephemeral divine.

        An earthquake could shake the ocean
forcing waves to tumble over the seashore,
and the beachgoers,
would panic scream and roar

            with the fury of the sun,
        or a global pandemic,
        an untethered corona arch explodes.

        However that beast comes to me,
            Death will be welcomed
        after living my life at this speed,

I am a manic,
and good heavens
bring no good grief,

a manic in this life,
I will dig in deeper to this life
than you ever could believe,

and slingshot out like a bullet
                    rippling sounds
            so fast that they screech,

a bang in the dark,
a pop through reality
gridlines will shift
        when I peak,

an extension of my creator,
        I'll do better
than what I would see,

when I peered carelessly
        into the dark pit,
        in my rock bottom moments
when my real persona
        was revealed to me,

everything I know
that lives inside of me,
        so dark and so deep,

        is not allowed to interject here,
I keep those visions all locked away
                and out of reach,

because my life will be
        one of lightness
        and beauty.

        But I am no better
than the one who gambled away his life earnings
in the heat of poker-faced passionate disgrace,

        I am no better
than the one who died in the ambulance,
his heart exploding from the years of bodily abuse,

        I am no better
than the homeless man
who talks to imaginary beings,
from places that coexist beyond your belief,

I have just learned
how to keep my fuel
from catching aflame,

I use my bottomless mania
when life has me down to my final chip,
but I believe in myself more than my God

so I never feel afraid,
I have risen from rock bottom
like a phoenix burning with life gone aflame,

I am navigating games of passion
        with some precaution,
so I don't burn everything else away,

but I'm reaching for the gas every now and then
        so I can see things glow
            in the most beautiful arrays.

a Poolside Scene

"Kick him out!"
I scream in my head,

The man has gone crazy,
they must kick him out;
he is too dangerous to be left out here,
in all of his belligerent screaming,
        he needs to go to bed!

he is throwing his oversized glass
        it shatters on the floor
and cuts his leg open to a gash,

he stumbles over the pool chair
and takes a slippery fall
        down to reality and it is better for us all,

they are dragging him out; he isn't putting up a fight
he coughs up his daiquiri, all over his tropical shirt,
                a kiwi green delight

throw him in bed; he has got things to work out
his nightmares are coming from this immature bout,

everyone is relieved,
but I don't want him to feel ashamed,

it has been a bad fucking year,
at some point in the last few months,
we've all felt the same

a moment of empathy
a drunken momentary slip this year,
isn't overly insane

the party must go on
life moves now, in different ways

I am thankful for every day
that I have been counting,
each day
since everything in this world
had changed.

Lizard Heat

They're playing a little melody over the radio,
a 1950's crooner song, where the notes are played
                    with symbols and kazoos,

            the poolside restaurant is empty
because it recently re-opened for business,
the waiter is pitching their rewards program
I am just thirsty, and with nothing else to do.

It is the right kind of town,
the summer brings extreme heat.
            80 degrees at sundown in October,
I forgot my sandals by the pool chair
so when I walked over the hot concrete
            I nearly burnt my feet.

It is the kind of year where you want to stay inside,
            everyone is wearing masks now
            and the pool is emptier than it used to be,
 I ordered some Jack and peach tea,
a plate of blueberry and watermelon,
            without the seeds,
            the salad has strawberries,
and I forgot to bring the heavy SPF sunscreen,

this music still tinkering all over,

echoing in the air
buzzing in my ears, Buddy holly
is sounding like Vampire Weekend,

I am a lizard in the sun rays,
the saguaros stand still as the jets fly over us
and this fall, feeling like a summer, weathered scene,

life is better this year
because it has boiled my choices down
to what is most important
to me.

Until it Stops Too

Sometimes my heart feels so full,
I am pretty sure that it is going to give out,

it feels so full
of gratitude,

but I feel unworthy
of all of its beats

it feels so full
it could explode
at any moment,

I am pretty sure
I will fall as it combusts,

but it never has; I move
a hundred pounds every minute,

my heart feels heavy and full,
but I bring it with me fully

never sure of its next beat
or my next step,

I move anyway,

and my heart moves too

I will not stop
until it stops
too.

Flamingo

She puts on her indigo necklace;
the one she used to wear with the band,
         her oversized sun hat,
with those ridiculous cat eye sunglasses
covering up half of her face,

her heels click
when she walks,
to the mirror
and smiles like a star
swinging her hips
when she turns for the door,

         change was what was left,
in the smallest pocket of last season's swimming suit,
                  two coins
                  in the candy machine
                          that dispensed the fish food,
                  outside of the Koi fish pond,

         she let the quarters roll
round and round before releasing,
we hear it rattling between her words
before the food drops out to the cup below.

Standing outside,
waiting for the sun to drop
her arms are crossed, leaning over the railing
with this grapefruit colored sunset showing,

over the ledge of the pond,
wishes
that she threw out of her hands,
down to the water right below,
feeding the fish, one wish
one fish
at a time,
with nothing else
needing to be tossed
or flipped by fate.

A cell phone flashlight turned on
to light up the darkened balcony,
the world is hers to take
delicate hands,
dropping the food
into small splashes
and big fish gulps,

I could stay here forever,
this fuzzy music is still flowing in
from the other side of the mountain range,
wishes spoken aloud

ripple in the tall glasses of water
we didn't drink,
because we foolishly bought the extra large,
horchata milkshakes.

Club Your Heart, (Desert Dream #2)

He tried to club your heart, that jack of spades,
      and you still look at him
      with your rose-colored shades,
      but those diamond looks
      are just another masquerade,
and shining, eternal youth, yeah, it too will fade.

      You've got to know yourself
before you slide on that golden ring,
      a precious loop holding
the burdening shock of everything,
awakening all sorts and suits of shuffled up truths,
      you had to experience;
for love this shiny and new.

You don't always get a hand in hearts
you aren't promised a seat in the game,
it is all much stronger than chance;
You've got to start with a round of solitaire first,
a single twinkling light in the spread of Milky Ways.

      Because when the heart is skewed
darkness can expand across everything in view,
you say this is love as big as the night sky,
but I, too, can agree to disagree with you.

You are all in and so bold;
this game will unfold
not when the river card is exposed
but when the twisting of words
begin to fold over time,
        like a tape tangled up in rewind,

you will need a spindled pencil twist,
to undo the mess that was made,
in that old car, with those words that he said
the first time that he drove away.

        Just put the cassette back in, hit play,
close your eyes, and let the music carry you away,
that big band of stars is there,
marvel in this display, be brave enough
to hear the subtler notes this time,
as his taillights begin to fade.

        Younger love, please know,
        you are better than okay
        but an ace of hearts does not ever
        appear and disappear this way,

a shooting star burns down the windshield
because gravity is too strong
for that fire not to be made,

you will find love again, but next time
your heart won't end up burning
         from the fervid beats being played.

Morning Tea

I was born in the sunrise
but I grow in all seasons
an electric tingle from my head to my toes,

I am a visionary; I can see things remotely
and influence the way that they unfold,

in harmony with my destiny,
I live this life deep in desires, bold

        adding warm water,
the tea empties from the bag
in this holiday peppermint candy flow,

next the milk and honey,
it starts to soothe my sore throat,

        a child of all seasons
I embrace each day as it unfolds,

I create with purpose and duty,
like reality is dependent on the way
that my thoughts show,

exposing myself was a powerful moment
the tea is still spiraling this year's pillowing growth,

my dreams are much bigger now,
I hold this in my hands and head toward the
window,

my mind flies towards the south
        soaring now,
I allow parts of me to go

these feelings may return to me someday,
but they will return much more beautiful

        because
        I allowed myself
            this growth.

the Wild

There is no turning back.
I am too deep in the wild.

I choose to be lost.
       I choose to explore.

       I know less and less,
       the further that I go.

I am lost in the woods now.

       What exists in front of me
are big dreams from this wildlife,
and the beasts of the wild world
           that surrounds.

the Hills Will Shake

Tell it to the cacti
yell it up the limestone hill,
    the dried out river bed
welcomes the early sunrise chill,

we drive the rental car up the mountain
and lose the signal on the radio,
the big trumpeting accordion
fades into snow-capped hills,

I am not sure how these tires will do
    on the little Chevy sedan,
    on the route of the middleman,
it is rocky roads from here to heaven,

I just want some big mountain air
    and high altitude cooking,
    the views are stunning now
but the drop-offs make my body shake,
        some leftover anxiety
from the stress I thought I had left behind,

    I left my watch at the hotel
so I don't have to remember the time,
    big Arizona skies,
open their arms to Mexico,

a hawk is circling the car now
and wild turkeys are running around,

the high altitude cookies are enormous here
I am going to feel sick on the drive back down,
       windy roads forever,
this life is just another sunny day,
it shines out warmth so gently,

       everything can be so subtle
       that you could miss it all
if you don't lift your head every now and then,
and take a good look around.

A Classic Car

Passionate light
red and bright,
it blinks to green,
and I rev the engine
in this dream machine,

It rattles on the turns
power steering fluid burned,
an orange classic Ford car
feels hot with electricity on the hood,

      motor muffling screech,
      stuttering speech,
it is hard to hear over the engine,
the radiator could overheat,

the food at the hotel is awful,
      we went out for a drive-through horchata
to sip down with the chile rellenos
we brought back to eat by the pool,
      our plastic silverware snaps
when I try to cut it into those peppers,

It is a vacationed dream,
this whole year is an escape
I have shed my worries

and I try to feel, try not to think,
       I feel out the day
one moment at a time,
only a rough idea of what to do
pulling moment
       by moment,
from the universal mind

there is a plan for me,
I am only just discovering it
because I have decided
       to see this life
all the way through.

the Final Days

Perfect Destruction

Skip and stop,
recover and protect the chambers,
just two loving buds
thorny stem and bloody drops.

Up and down,
cardiac arrest and drop,
a seismograph of feelings
big beats and my heartaches
echoing shots.

You can't fake it,
can't make it stop,
my heart jumps around,
and I am not who I thought.

My heart detonates,
a giant mushroom cloud of doubt,
that perfect destruction,
was something I could not stop.

*The news that came was nothing
I had considered was possible.*

Our Park Blanket

Our picnic blanket, that old gas station throw
has stains from the porter spilled
     on the Fourth of July
     just a few summers ago,

the park is only partially open,
the grass is very moist and green,
the playground is caution taped over
but there is nowhere else for us to be,

I am craving a coffee from Carson's
and memory's of those old study dates,
the world was so much simpler then,
     no backup masks to carry
or so many reasons to feel afraid,

       we had our first baby
and thought that we would try again,
but those dreams were miscarried
without consideration that
     that could happen,

     no son for now
the starry skyline is coming in,
this blanket can only keep so much warmth
before we start shivering,

it is time to head back to the hotel
I have got Topo Chico's on ice,
it is probably best to stay sober
      on the kind of feelings,
        that we are feeling tonight.

Empty Sting

When it's a secret,
you aren't allowed to be sad,
when you can't tell anyone
it is so much harder to
        let go,

but it's a harsh thing
        this empty sting

I could see him
with that southern charm,
        a big steady heart,
always caring for his mom,

so It's a hard pill to swallow,
this empty thing,
        this echoing sting,

I remember that night at the dinner table;
when we knew he was not going to be coming,

        It was a tearful night,
        a big and empty sting,

he told me he couldn't settle in,
he was sorry for everything,

I told him we'd be ready
if he was to try again,

but I don't hear him as I did before,
I keep feeling this empty sting,

      maybe when I'm older
he will come back to me,
and I can share these dreams
with him and Penelope,

I am ready to see them both,
      and let go of the sting
      this heavy, empty sting.

Key Lime Pie Slice(s)

The electric guitar strums
in the corner of the balcony,
I sit waiting for my waitress to bring us the tab
       I have got a wallet full of change
        but the old arcade is closed for now,
        they've got too many contact points
          to be sanitized every hour,
with all of the knobs, buttons, and screens.

There is an antique shop with clothes
meant for the drag dress up across the street,
I still have Hamburger Mary's memories,
I feel like a quarter pounding Royale with cheese,
       I have got dollars to throw
           and ways to escape
        this service takes forever
when they are operating on a fifth of the staff,
a third of the visitors they usually see,
the chef is ready to clock out
by day he is a poolside burger boy
and by night, she's a full patty queen.

Electric shakes and drum set shaped cakes,
a picture of the Monkees on the wall,
but their autographs look fake
I am rolling in with sunglasses tonight,

67

this look is fitting me well,
it's such a strange cosmic place.

The waitress asks
what made us want to come to Arizona,
"Well, we are driving to the vortex in the morning,
and hanging out for the binocular UFO tour
when the sun sets at night,"

She will be ready to break for LA
or somewhere to dream away
when she has got enough money saved,
staring at the hazy heat too long
can make this place feel dusty barren, dry,
and without a moment of shade.

I am tucking into my flamingo pink sweatshirt hood,
squawking at the saguaros in the parking lot,
"Two key lime pie slices to go, please,"
we just need plastic silverware,
and a few napkins, so we don't ruin my off white vans
that I bought earlier in the day.

We will eat them on the evening hike to the waterfall,
outside of the property, yes,
it seems everyone, including us,
is ready for the next escape.

I've got it Good

I've got it good
that's why I don't tempt fate
there are decades and lifetimes
full of mistakes that I have made,
     with all of my past lives
that I have taken to my grave,
I have no choice now but to stay here
even when I am feeling homesick and afraid.

One world of many
one life to live right now,
     thoughts pillowing
     with feelings abound,
erupting in the depths under me,

there are things I can't explain
     but they are there,
     not in vain,
     no, they are there
like my destiny is preordained,
and I am thankful when I see them
     moving toward me,
     on days like yesterday
     and today.

Burning

Big courage takes
warm flames
fiery in my gut
to burn me down,

a steady strength,
tall stance
in my frame,
to hold me up

big breathes
that fill and hold me,
there's always so much
for me to release,

I exhale the past,
          air escapes
and time passes me by,
making room for grace.

Grateful patience,
chaos embraced
big bravery,
I can hold this space,

something new

is happening and that's okay,
I've got belief to show

things will grow,
feelings change
I'm letting them go
and balancing lightly,

I'm just a rock
holding water,
I let it flow
over and under me,

I'm moving too
I'm growing tall,
certain of uncertainty,
and not sure who I used to be

I'm a warm belly
of fiery peace,
pieces of everything
I'm trying to be,

go dancing around
I let them settle
and don't think much
on how they're supposed to be,

I am confident,
my best confidante
is there inside of me,
burning bright and ready to be.

Twinkle Twinkle

Twinkle twinkle pixie night
butterfly colors, flashes of flapping sights

neon flowers are swelling to bloom
and to half-life decay,
we are at max capacity,
don't forget your mask tonight,

we head into the shower curtained restaurant booth,
hand sanitizer stands are dripping to the ground.

You deserve that pineapple margarita
and I'm tipping the waitress well when we leave,

I do not want any more noises
going off in my head,

this churro ice cream is smooth,
and it's laying down my dreams in that blue
blanketed hotel bed,

twinkle twinkle stars surround,
no pollution from the city lights,

I see something trail across the sky now
a parade of Star Link satellites,

it makes you wonder
about the years we face ahead,

I wish for responsible decision-making,
when these visions of fleeing the state go flashing in
my head,

of a ranch style home in the desert,
solar panels to power the machines,

I hear a gentle whisper
a twinkling trail of time leading toward my future,

someday I will live in this valley,
stars are radiating this distant light year heat,

red and yellow flickering balls of the cosmos
putting holes in the dark sheets of the sky,

they twinkle above the car
and my desert blooming heart
flutters distant wishes,
out to the cosmic sea.

Spatially Aware

Flashes of sun drip
I am spatially aware,
big orange flares hold steady in the sky

beacons holding location, movements, and emotion
        like a piano concerto,
            or something orchestrated out of thin air,

                beacons over an open plane
or a receptacle of energy, holding high in the sky
            above stone faces and chemicals unknown,

            call me for the directions to get here,
this place is just another corner of the world
            I call home,

tonight is just another scene in the dream machine,
projecting life as a continuous stream of events
            where I do not think
we could ever exist in the giant sea of space
            as a solitary spinning home,

            no....
we have cosmic neighbors
        visiting this place,
            and we are not alone.

the Neighbors

The sky has a dent in it tonight,
            I see
        the ceiling folding in,

            I hear them
the voices of those stars, big spheres of energy,
        waves of emotions washing along
                my closed eyelids,

        maybe I should get my eyes checked,
there is a red and blue sparkling point up there,
it looks like Mars until it disappears
            red to black,

yeah, the star energy is here,
beings of light, beings of body
        they are here too,

I can't help but know they are here,
because I feel them inside of me
        vibrating musical sounds
        and wild frequencies,

            I am alive,
        we are all the same,
life is just the force that is inside of this frame,

that works this mind,
beings of creation,

I am just a garden blooming,
            we are a garden growing,
sometimes I am not sure if we are growing
                        or being grown,
            but we are magic,
      we are still human,
      we are here and there
light-years, light feelings abound

            we are all the same,
      a gentle knowing,
      that life is buzzing near us
      stars teeming with life,
                  surround.

Floodlight the Present

Some take their time
putting things into place,
maybe a few times over a decade,

but life has been moving too fast for me,
I feel like every year, I am someone different
and I have this unyielding curiosity,

like a funnel or spiral of colors
opening in the sky
or a swirling galaxy,

a million points of light
flood and spin towards me,
they've been up there forever,
ready for their discovery

life moves relentlessly,
me and my giant head
floating away as a red balloon on a string,

I'll get lost in the clouds
and lift into some gulf stream of consciousness,
pulling me to eternity,

I'm a hopeless romantic

a dreamer living in this dreamland,
the world is pure magic and majesty,

I'll lift for a little while
and write down what I see,
things move so quick at times,

but I can move fast like lightning
shaking the clouds into separate pieces,
only to swirl back together in a boom,

just a dark, ominous re-positioning
I shock myself bright as the daylight,
        in the night
I sparkle and crackle over the mile-high mountains,

sloshing everything to the valley floor
washing the car's headlights out on the desert streets,
        I will floodlight the present
        because I want it to
        show something of importance
                        to me.

Saguaro Country

To know the secrets of this land
you have to run the trails,
read the movement of the water
and tell the stories
       left in the desert sand,

       this is saguaro country
where the puncturing cacti
       outnumber the pines,
a forest of uniquely, poisonous growth
and prickly clouds
       that spiral over the skyline,

where sand covers the limestone
and my feet
       sink in way too deep,
every step higher is a near slip, fall
and scrape over rocks
       too treacherously steep.

I run down the trail
       like water,
flowing over old memories
the hills they whisper in the back row
of silent movie theater dreams,
       in an old western

a cowboy nearing the mountain tops
            with only that water
                        in his pouch,

that image flashes in
            its modern equivalent match,
a motorcycle revving up the windy road
a renegade rendezvous
            is that same solo ride of now,

            a ninja,
went flying up the windy mountain
he crashes on the asphalt,
            during his trip back down,
death can be unforgiving
in the desert of the south,

the scene is simply awful
as we drive past it
            I force myself
to close my chattering mouth

            flowers will still blossom
in the dark of the valley at night,
            with stars that seem too milky
for these city lights that surround,

            my daughter

sleeps in the queen sized hotel bed,
        not quite ready
                for her birthday tomorrow
        this trip
        will be ending soon enough,
the wide arm jet will hug
        the hills of the south,

        the secrets of the land
are just riddles we can't find,
there are tall green spine statues everywhere
        in the saguaro desert night,

all that I will have from this trip
are spiral visions
        of forest green army stoicism,
        windy road, cactus stinging
        heated bouts of thirstiness,
and heavy visions regarding the past
                and future
                of man.

the Projector Plays

I never did any hard drugs
because there was no need

I'm already a firefly, a lava lamp
glowing when I'm charged,
flickering through the night
little buzzes near and far,

      I am already addicted to my emotions
to my dreams, and to manifesting summer blossoms
      from spring's hopeful seeds,

I am so eager to shine like a fucking star,
         I glow in the dark
      when the sun goes down
      and it's too dark to believe,

I could have been dead by now,
burning like a meteor
a silent stream bright and beautiful,
      disappearing so quick
you would have had to question
what you had seen,

my mind is already a collection of space junk,
      a wormhole of mystery

spiraling out of perception,
so sacred and so free

drugs would've killed me
but I chose to be in this body
and live out the remainder
    of this dream,

    a prisoner to promise
an unfettered stream of consciousness
    through my vision machine
    I am projecting
    out onto this stage
    illuminated in front of me.

Home

I am heading home
but not where I want to be,

this life feels like a performance,
an act that carries on for a while
                              as a lucid dream

I will head home and go over
the lessons that I have learned,

              in this story
              in this scene

I used to believe I was the black sheep
but now I know the truth,
         I am the dark horse
setting out to scratch everything
that I feel itching inside of me,

the universe is under your spell
and working for you too,
it will reinvent its same lessons
until you own their truths,

              it likes to whisper
              it likes to scream,

it likes to tickle and torment you
            with its teachings
            in in the most beautiful
            of idiosyncrasies,

        I head home
each time I close my eyes,
I am inching closer
to the things I can see
rising inside of me,

            I am lifting in the sky
on a gasoline bird stretching out its wings,
everything in view is speeding away from me

I will stay present as long as the dream proceeds
            because big maybes are visible everywhere,
            and big decisions are still here in front of me.

            I choose to tune in
            so I can pull closer
            to what I want
            and what I need,
            I am tuning in
            to a higher frequency

I am learning that
in the end,

I am a collection
        of feelings
that remain
inside of me,

I am a spirit from the sky,
        living
        in a hazy,
        wild and raw
vacationed dream.

This is the end.

Thank you for reading.

www.ingramcontent.com/pod-product-compliance
Lightning Source LLC
Chambersburg PA
CBHW071829020426
42331CB00007B/1664